India is my country

In this book 28 people from all over India tell you what their life is like — life in the overcrowded cities, life in the village and life in the factory.

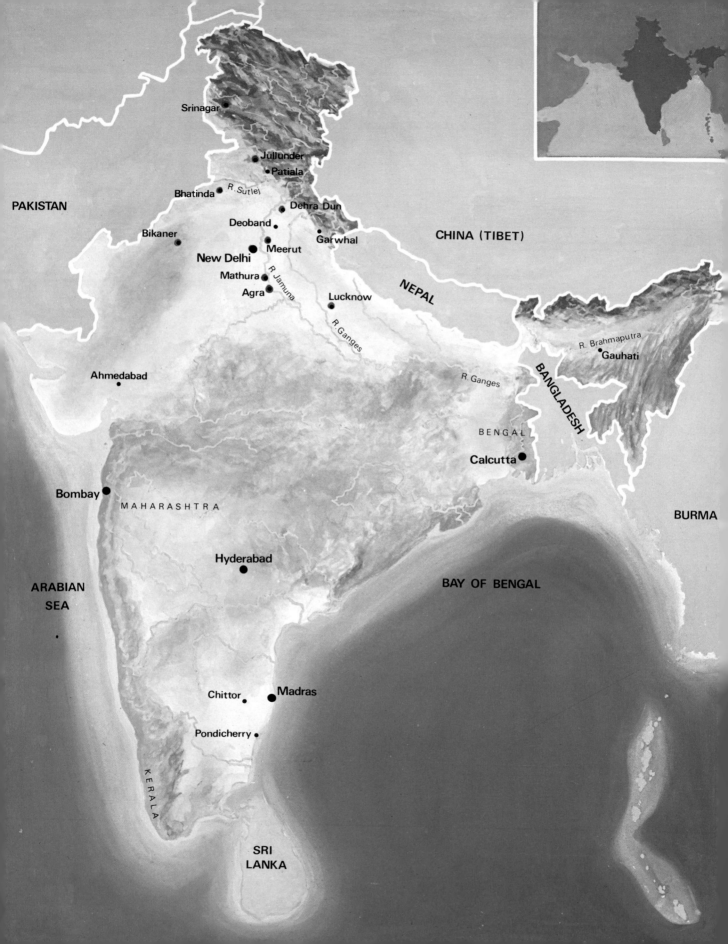

INDIA
is my country

Cliff and Bernice Moon

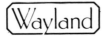

My Country

America is my country
Australia is my country
Britain is my country
China is my country
Denmark is my country
France is my country
Greece is my country
India is my country
Israel is my country
Italy is my country
Kenya is my country
New Zealand is my country
Spain is my country

Further titles are in preparation

*This book is based on an original text by
Veenu Sandal and photographs by Brahm Dev*

First published in 1983 by
Wayland (Publishers) Ltd.
49 Lansdowne Place, Hove
East Sussex BN3 1HF, England

© Copyright 1983 Wayland (Publishers) Ltd

Second impression 1985

ISBN 0 85078 323 2

Phototypeset by VDU Characters Ltd.,
Burgess Hill, Sussex, England

Printed by G. Canale & C. S.p.A., Turin, Italy
Bound in the U.K. by The Pitman Press, Bath

Contents

My name is Ram and I sell fruit.

Would you like to eat a nice juicy melon, some grapes
or a pomegranate?
I sell all kinds of fruit on my stall.
In the summer I sell mangoes. They are delicious and cheap.
I also sell apples, oranges, pineapples, bananas,
plums, coconuts, cherries and raspberries.
I get up at 5.00 a.m. every morning.
I have a quick bath and a cup of tea.
I walk to the nearest market to buy my fruit.
Then I take the fruit back to my stall.
Many of my Indian customers like eating fruit for lunch
so they do their shopping early in the morning.

Here are some people
buying vegetables from
a vegetable stall.
There are no prices
on the vegetables.
Customers argue with the
stall-holder and agree
on a price.

I like to take a break at lunchtime because a fruit seller's day
is very long. I stay at my stall until 9 o'clock at night.
All day I weigh out fruit, argue about the prices and
watch the people going past.

This is my wife.
She is called Bimpa and
she is grinding flour.
She cooks over a wood fire
even on a hot day.

7

I am Shanker and I am a postman.

How does the post get to your house?
Does it come in a van, on a bike or does someone carry it?
When I deliver the post I ride my camel!
My camel and I have to travel across the desert and
carry the post to remote village people.
If we did not take the post to them they would have to walk
for miles and miles across the desert for it.

Here is a village in the desert.
The people are pleased
to see me and someone
always comes out to meet us.

8

The people where I live
love dancing.
These dancers are dressed
in wedding clothes.

Can you imagine what it is like to travel across a desert?
A camel postman's life is far from easy.
Sometimes I have to ride through blinding sand storms.
The wind and the sand make an awful moaning sound.
That is when I feel most frightened.
My camel and I are out there all alone.
But whatever happens the camel postman must always ride on
and deliver the post.

I am Randhir
and I am a prince.

I have plenty of money and I spend a lot of my time shooting.
I have been in the shooting events in five Olympic Games but
I still haven't won an Olympic medal.
I would love to win a medal for my country so
I just keep on practising.

Here I am at home
with my wife, Uma,
and my dog, Rusty.
We have eight servants
to do our cooking
and cleaning.

10

I used to shoot tigers when I was a boy but now
this has been stopped because
wildlife in India is protected.

I spend a lot of my time trying to improve sport in India.
We are trying to get better training and equipment
for everyone who enjoys sport.
I have quite a busy life because I have to practise my shooting
and I mustn't forget my business and farms.
They have to be looked after too!

I am Shivani and I am a student.

I am 18 years old and I am a student in Bengal.
I am studying Indian history and in two years' time,
if I pass my examinations, I will get my degree.
There are 118 universities in India but 20 years ago
there were only 47 universities.
In the smaller towns men and women students go to
separate colleges because of old Indian religious rules.
Young men and women are not allowed to mix freely.
However this is changing and in large universities like mine
young men and women students can study together.
In India there are no grants for students so my parents
must pay for everything.

This is one of the
colleges where both men
and women students can
study and relax together.

This student is making
a study of pictures
painted by people
in Indian villages.

13

I am Maharaj and I look after old buildings.

My job is looking after old statues and buildings.
Broken statues have to be repaired and I have to look
for stone and marble that was used a long time ago.
I am always trying out new ways of repairing the stone.

What is happening
to this old statue?
The stone is slowly
crumbling away.
More and more factories ▶
are being built in India.
The smoke and dirt in the air
attack the stone and
make it crumble.

This is a famous old monument in India.
People used to watch the stars from here
hundreds of years ago.

If you look for Agra on the map of India
you will see where I live.
In Agra there is a very famous building called the *Taj Mahal*.
It is one of the most beautiful buildings in the world.
There are always lots of tourists, especially at night,
because the Taj Mahal looks wonderful by moonlight.

I am Sanjay and I am a schoolboy.

This woman comes from the state of Kashmir where I live.
People say that the most beautiful women in India come from Kashmir.

I live in Srinagar, the capital of Kashmir, in the north of India.
My father pays for me to go to school so he expects me
to work hard and pass my exams.

I go to school from 7.00 a.m. until 1.00 p.m. in summer and
in the winter I go from 9.00 a.m. until 3.00 p.m.
My school is just like yours but not all schools
are like this in India.
In some parts of India you would have lessons outside
under the shade of trees.

You would enjoy going to school in Srinagar because
we don't have many roads.
Instead of roads we have waterways.
People live in houseboats and we have a floating post-office,
floating gardens and floating market-places.
Even weddings take place in a boat on the water!

My name is Kamal.
I am a policeman.

I joined the police force five years ago and I had no idea how busy I was going to be.

I have had to chase armed bandits, catch pick-pockets, break up fights, trap thieves, guard prisoners, go to court and control crowds.

I also have to check that bullock carts are not overloaded!

This is a law court.
It is built under large trees
so that people can work
in the shade.

I don't carry a gun but I do have a long wooden stick.
Like most policemen, we have radios, radar and dogs to help us.
Sometimes we need them!
One evening I set off with five other policemen on patrol.
Everywhere was peaceful until, at 8.30 p.m.
we went round a bend in the river and
ran straight into a group of people.
It was very dark so we couldn't see who they were.
Suddenly they started firing their guns at us!
We threw ourselves to the ground and luckily no-one was hit.
Later we chased them and caught one of them.
They had been stealing electric wires.
I was given an award for being so brave.

I am Hardwari and I am a priest.

My day at the temple begins at 4.30 a.m.
and ends at 8 o'clock at night.
I am a Hindu priest and a lot of Indian people are Hindus.
We don't believe in just one God but in many Gods.

This is a bridegroom
at a Hindu wedding.
He wears a crown
and he has flowers
round his neck.

Hindus believe that there is a God who made the world,
a God who looks after the world and
a God who destroys the world.
Then there are lots of other Gods and Goddesses.
There is a monkey God, an elephant-faced God
and a Goddess who rides a tiger.

This is a God
who has a face
like an elephant.
Priests pray to the God.
We wash the God
with milk and honey
and then we dress it.
You can also see
that the temple walls
are very beautiful.
This one has *mosaic*
patterns all over it.

I am Mr Munusamy and I am a Member of Parliament.

I have been in politics for 28 years now and
during this time I have travelled all round India.
Every day I meet people and listen to their problems.
Many Indians can't read or write and many are very poor.
Another big problem is that we have a very large population.
If we don't ask people to have smaller families
we will not have enough food to go round.
In spite of our problems we are one of the top
industrial countries in the world.
I am very proud to be an Indian and very happy
to serve my country as a Member of Parliament.

My home is in Pondicherry
which is near the sea.
Here is my family
watching the sunset
over the sea. ➡

This is a meeting
at election time.
Indians are very interested
in politics.
They talk for hours
at a meeting like this.
⬇

My name is Madan and I am a driver.

What do you think I drive?
It is an *auto-rickshaw* which is a kind of taxi.
It has three wheels and it is driven by a motorbike engine.
I borrowed money from the bank to buy it and
it took me five years to pay back the bank!

Would you like a ride?
It's cheaper than
an ordinary taxi but
dearer than a bus.
The trouble is, if you
see a bus it will
probably be full and
you won't get a seat.

If you look for Garwhal on the map of India
you will see where I drive my auto-rickshaw.
In Garwhal there are some very beautiful mountains.

Driving in Garwhal can be a problem because
there are no traffic signals or separate lanes.
Many people walk everywhere and they will not
get out of the way for an auto-rickshaw driver.
Then there are the cows!
Cows are very special animals in India.
No one will hurt them or push them.
Sometimes they lie down in the middle of the road and
there is nothing I can do.
I just have to stop and use my horn.
I've waited ages for a cow to get out of my way!

25

I am Padam and I collect books.

When I was a boy I wondered how I could get to know everything about India.

India is a very large country and many different kinds of people live here.

I decided to get to know India and her people by buying lots of books and reading them.

I live in Agra where you will find this famous building called the *Taj Mahal.*

I began buying books when I was young and now
I have a very large collection in my house.
As you can see I need a big house to store all my books.
In fact my house has twelve rooms!

Every year I add new books to my collection and
many people come to use the books in my library.
They come from all over India.
I read nearly all day long and usually
I read about 40 books a month.
I am very interested in the old days.
There have been people living in India for thousands of years.
Some of the things people do and believe nowadays
started years and years ago.
That's what I like to read about most of all —
how India and her people became what they are today.

I am Mohammed.
I own a factory.

I opened my factory six years ago.
We make tools like bench vices and we also make
brass doorknobs and nameplates.
I sell these things to countries all over the world.
We sell to the United States, Canada, West Germany,
Sweden, Australia and the Middle East.
Fifty people work at my factory but some factories
in India are much bigger than that.
Factories that make cloth from cotton are very big.
There are also factories which make iron, steel,
chemicals and heavy machines.
And we make our own cars, aeroplanes, trains,
ships, scooters and motorbikes.

Many of my friends play polo which is a favourite sport
of Indian people who are rich.

When I am not working in my factory I play squash
or ride my motorcycle.
I am crazy about motorcycles and love to break speed records!
I live with my family in a very large bungalow
which we share with my brother's family.
We have three servants, two cars and two motorcycles.

Here I am with my
youngest daughter.

My name is Abdul and I am a medicine man.

I am 96 years old and I have helped a lot of sick people by using old medical cures.
I have learnt all about bones so I often help people who have broken a bone or have put a bone out of joint.

Here I am with my family.
I have four sons and many grandchildren. ➤

This is a *mosque* and, as I am a Muslim,
I worship at a mosque like this.

Muslims often come to me for help but so do many other people.
If a person is poor, I charge very little for my cures,
but if they are rich, then I charge more.
I don't use medicines or tablets.
Instead I use the right kinds of herbs or oils.
For example, I treat deep cuts and wounds by putting
on a mixture of mustard oil and *turmeric* powder.
Turmeric is the stem of a plant which I grind into a powder.
Sick people can be cured in many different ways and
my ways have been used for thousands of years.

My name is Janu. I am the headman of my tribe.

I live in a thatched hut in the middle of a thick forest.
We live a long way from a city or town.
Last year I went to a city and
saw a train for the first time in my life.

This is my son.
He is playing an
instrument called a *tarpa*.
When the people hear it
they will come out and
start dancing.

Many people in India live in tribes like mine.
They all live far away from towns or cities.
My tribe grows rice and we have a lot of work to do.
We plough the rice fields, put in new rice plants
and fence the fields.
Everyone in our tribe has a job to do.
Our wives and daughters sometimes help in the fields and
they also grind the rice grain.
We make delicious pancakes from our rice grain.

In our spare time we like to make wood carvings
or weave mats and baskets which we sell to traders.

I am Narendar.
I am a farmer.

Yes, I am a farmer.
I use a tractor for ploughing the fields.
Behind my tractor you can see some bullocks.

The bullocks help with
the ploughing too.
We use modern and
old ways of farming
in India.

Just like farmers all over the world
I am always watching the weather.
Sometimes there is not enough rain and
all my crops dry up.
Sometimes there are floods and then
everything gets washed away.
But things are changing because now
I can also get water from my wells.
Not all Indian farmers are as lucky as me.
We grow sugar cane, wheat, rice, maize, cotton,
potatoes, vegetables, fruit, tea and coffee.
There are a lot of people in India and we try to grow
as much food as we can so that they will have enough to eat.

These children live in
a hut in the village
near my farm.

I am Hanuman.
I teach wrestling.

I am 81 years old but I can still show you how to wrestle!
I started wrestling when I was 7 years old.
Wrestling has been a favourite sport in India
for thousands of years.
Many young people in India would like to be wrestling heroes.
Other Indian sports are archery and chess but
nowadays we play football, cricket and tennis as well.

Here are two of my
young pupils.

They are practising
in a mud pit.

This is Hanuman,
the Hindu monkey-god.
I was named after him.

Come to my school and learn how to wrestle!
At present I am training 500 wrestlers and
most of them are aged from 5 to 15 years.
The daily timetable is very strict and we get up very early.
We have a quick wash and massage and then we're off —
racing, doing our exercises, lifting weights and
climbing ropes.
We choose our food very carefully and eat a lot of vegetables.
My teaching must be good because in 1960
one of my boys was sent to the Olympics in Rome.
Most of the time the boys practise in mud pits but
we also have a very expensive foam mat.
I only let the very best wrestlers use it.
There are just two other mats like it in India.

I am Phulki and I am a blacksmith.

My husband, Dhulia, is a blacksmith like me.
We travel all over India in our little cart home.
When we stop we set up our furnace and start to make
all the tools that village people need.

Here I am with my friends
getting ready to dance
at a wedding.

My husband is making
some tools and my sister is
looking after the furnace.
Our children have to travel
everywhere with us.

We make pick-axes, sickles for cutting rice and
all kinds of cooking pans.
If any of these things are broken we will mend them.
Of course, most of what we earn is spent on food.
Our favourite meals are lamb or chicken curry and boiled eggs
and, like many Indians, we drink a lot of tea.
We spend the rest of our money on clothes and silver jewellery.
I'm very fond of jewellery as you can see.

I am Shib Dayal.
I am a zookeeper.

I know you would like my job but how would you like to kiss a white tiger?
My life is one big adventure at New Delhi Zoo.
I have more than 3,000 animal friends!

This is the white tiger who kisses me!
He is called Moti and he is 2 years old.

42

Of course, if you are a zookeeper you are kept very busy.
I have 60 keepers to help me feed and look after the animals.
Sometimes the work is very dangerous.
A tiger escaped once and unfortunately we had to shoot it.
Another day 17 monkeys escaped but we managed
to get them all back safely.
It is all in a day's work for me but each time
I was given awards for bravery.

This Langur monkey
likes to eat *guavas*.
He doesn't always sit
still like this.
He was one of the
monkeys who escaped!

I am Rajinder and I direct plays.

Do you like drama?
I acted in my first play when I was only 6 years old.
I don't act in plays any longer because now I am a director.

It is my job to tell
the actors what to do.
These actors are in
a scene from one
of my plays.

Plays have been acted in India for more than 2,000 years.
In the old days groups of actors travelled around
putting on plays in the village streets.
Most of the plays were based on our religious beliefs.
In most of the plays the good people always win over the bad.
It is exciting to see plays with colourful costumes,
drums and music.
Before a new play can be put on, the director has to work
very hard with his actors.

Here I am directing a rehearsal of a new play.

I am Ramaswami and I am a fortune teller.

Many Indians believe in luck and telling fortunes by the stars.
Sometimes I look at their hands to tell them
what will happen in the future.
I have two parrots to help me.
They hop out of their cages and pick up special cards.
Things that might happen in the future are written on the cards.

Can you see my parrot,
Tota, coming out
of his cage?
He will pick up a card
and the card will say
what is going to happen
to the woman.

46

A fortune teller is a very important person in India.
If people have some special work to do they go
to the fortune teller to see what he says about it.
When a new baby is born, the fortune teller will say
what kind of life the new baby will have.
Many marriages are decided by reading the stars.
Many Indians don't move into a new house or
start a new business until the fortune teller
tells them that the time is right.
So I have to read and study old charts very carefully.
My uncle showed me how to be a fortune teller and
I do everything he told me.
He also told me that it was the *Indian* way
of fortune telling which spread to China and other countries.

In the evenings, I like
to go to the races.
The horses pull carts
called *tongas.*

I am Praveen.
I am a film star.

If you look for Bombay on the map of India
you will see where my films are made.

This is the Taj Hotel in Bombay and
many tourists come to see it. ➡

This is one of the film stars
I work with.
She is very beautiful.

Indians love watching films and when I was a boy
I loved watching films too.
Now people watch *me* in the films!
When a new film is going to be shown everybody
gets to know about it.
Big posters are put up in large towns and
the newspapers print big adverts.
In the smaller towns men go around beating drums and
shouting through loud-speakers.
They make sure that everybody knows about the new film.
There are films about religion, children's films, thrillers and
films about family life.
The good people always win and the bad always lose in our films.
I like to be one of the good people so that I can win at the end!

I am Dipali and I am a railway worker.

I live in the very north of India at Gauhati.
There is one main railway line from Gauhati to Calcutta.
If you look on the map of India you will find Gauhati
and Calcutta.
The railway is called the North East Frontier Railway and
that is where I work.

Gauhati is in the
state of Assam.
In Assam there are
many elephants and ➤
sometimes we ride them.

I love dancing.
We often dance to
the music of drums.

I have to make sure that people or goods travelling
on the railway have a safe journey.
Most of the time the railway runs without any problems but
sometimes things go wrong.
A few months ago a train was eight hours late.
Could somebody have put a bomb on the train?
Had it been in an accident?
Can you guess what had happened?
It was late because of elephants!
The train driver and the passengers shouted at them but
the elephants would not move off the track.
So everyone had to wait until the elephants decided to go!

I am Jasbir Singh and I am a dressmaker.

Here I am with my family.
We are shopping at
the street market.
Do you like the dress
my wife is wearing?
My job is to make lovely
dresses for Indian women.

I make all my wife's dresses myself and
I choose the materials very carefully.

There is always someone who would like a new dress.
I have eight workers to help me because I get
so many orders.
Often we are all working far into the night
getting all our dresses finished.
We use the finest Indian cottons and, because cotton
is grown in India, it is very cheap.
Cotton clothes are cool in the hot weather we get in India.
If you look at my photograph you will see
that I am wearing a turban.
This is because I am a Sikh.
Sikhs never cut their hair so mine is tied up in a knot
on top of my head and I wrap my turban around the knot.

Sikhs like to go to the Golden Temple of Amritsar.
I have been there myself and, as you can see, it is very beautiful.

I am Atma Ram.
I am a potter.

Would you like a flower pot, a water jar or even a clay toy?
I can make one for you on my potter's wheel.

Here I am at work.
My wife and children
help me too.
How many pots do you
think I have made?

This is my wife.
She is called Bina Devi.
She carries my pots
on her head and
goes from house to house
trying to sell them.

I usually make about 600 pots a day.
Early in the morning I mix up all the clay that
I will need and then I start shaping pots on my wheel.
Lots of people come to watch me work in the hot sun.
Sometimes they buy the things I have made that day.
I finish work in the evening when the sun sets.
That is when I count the money I have made that day!

I am Salma Sultan and I am a TV newsreader.

I have been reading the news on Indian television for ten years.
When people meet me they often say,
'What an exciting job you've got.'
But really it's quite hard work.

Our country is the seventh largest in the world so
it has 18 television centres.
Many of our people can't read or write so
they watch television to find out the news.
A lot of our people can't afford a television of their own.
The government gives sets to the villages.
If you don't have a set of your own your friend
may have one and then you can watch together.
Indian people are very friendly and they always welcome strangers
into their homes.

Here are some of the
things I like to eat.
We live in Delhi
where we can buy
lots of different
kinds of food.
Sometimes we go out
to a Chinese restaurant
in the evening.

There are parades in India
on Republic Day every year.
They are always filmed and
shown on television.
The colourful costumes and
flags help to make
the television programmes
exciting to watch.

My name is K. Ramakrishnan and I am a magazine editor.

If you look on the
map of India you
will find Kerala.
That is where I work.
The people of Kerala
love flowers.
This woman goes
from house to house
selling her flowers.

Do you like reading comics or children's magazines?
Well, I am the editor of a magazine for children.

Kerala is by the sea.
The coast of Kerala
is famous for its
palm trees and coconuts.
How would you like
a coconut for breakfast?
In Kerala that is one of
our favourite breakfasts!

My magazine is written in English and it has
a little bit of everything in it.
We print a lot of old Indian folk tales.
There are thousands of old Indian stories.
Every Sunday I talk to children and find out
what they would like to read about in the next magazine.
Yes, I really think you would like to read my magazines.

I am Hira Lal.
I am an engineer.

This is the Bhakra Nangal Dam and it is the largest dam in India. The dam helps to make electricity and my job is to make sure the electricity gets to as many towns and villages as possible.

I wanted to be an engineer when I was at school.
It is a well paid job and India needs lots of engineers.
There are more than 20 large rivers in India and
we have 28 dams on them.
The dams control floods, make electricity and store water
so that farmers can water their crops.
At the moment I am very busy helping to plan and build
four new power stations.
Factories use most of the power so many villages
still don't have electricity.
Such a lot of our villages have to make do
with oil lamps, lanterns and candles.
It will take a long time to get electricity
to every home in a big country like India, but
I am working hard to make it happen.

I only eat fruit
and vegetables.
These are mangoes and
they are my favourite fruit.

Facts

Capital City   The capital city of India is New Delhi.

Language   Many people in India speak Hindi. English is used a lot and there are many other local languages.

Money   Indian people pay for things with paise and rupees. There are 100 paise in 1 rupee.

Religion   Most people in India are Hindus but there are also Muslims, Christians, Sikhs, Buddhists and Jains.

Weather   The weather in India can either be cool or very, very hot. In June and July there is very heavy rain called the monsoon rain.

People   There are over 650,000,000 people living in India. Each month 1,000,000 more babies are born.

Government   India doesn't have a king or queen. Instead the Indian people elect a President every five years.

Houses

This is a big problem in India.
In many houses there are 3 or 4
people living in one room.
There are too many people and
not enough houses for them.

Schools

Many people in India do not know
how to read and write because
they have never been to school.
However, things are changing and new
schools are being built all the time.

Farming

Farmers in India grow rice, wheat,
groundnuts, rape seed, mustard,
sesame seed, linseed, cotton, coffee,
sugar cane and tea.
Often their crops are damaged by
floods or by very dry weather.

News

Many people in India do not have
a radio or TV set.
Instead the government gives them
to villages and everybody gets together
to watch and listen to the news.

Index